OLD REMANATS
NEW BUDS

OLD REMANATS
NEW BUDS

KATHERINE STONE AYERS

Copyright © 2015 by Katherine Stone Ayers

All rights reserved.
Printed in the United States of America.
No part of this book may be reproduced
without the publisher's written permission.

Flowing Rivers Publications

ISBN-13: 978-0-9965968-5-5

ISBN-10: 0996596852

Enjoy Katharine's art at: www.katharinestoneayers.com

Cover and book design by Cherri LaMarr

Other Books by Katherine Stone Ayers

Trembling Heart

Opening

From Frozenness to Freedom

Dedication

To Allies:
Grandma Stone, Gibby,
Uncle Pie, Hannah

To the Grace that allows us
to open to Joy and Presence

Old Remnants – New Buds

Dear Poetry Lovers and Friends,

The poetry in this book emerged out of traumatic experiences I had in early life and the journey I took towards healing. Writing poetry was part of my healing. Grace and good fortune led me to resources I needed to heal my past. For me, it was and continues to be a miraculous, transformational journey.

Writing this book was fueled by my desire to let others know that healing is possible; we don't have to be stuck in old and limiting patterns.

For those of you who might want to use or take advantage of some or all of the resources I used to heal, I would like to give you a list of them:

1. Chiropractic
Chiropractic care provided profound healing of my physical body and inspired me to become a Chiropractor. Chiropractic philosophy teaches that Universal Intelligence manifests as Innate Intelligence in our body. When our physical structure is aligned by Chiropractic adjustments, nerve supply can move freely and Innate Intelligence can bring the body back into balance.

2. Somatic approaches
Studying and teaching Applied Kinesiology helped me realize that physical structure, physiology, body chemistry and emotions are intertwined and all affect our state of being.

Somatics and Feldenkrais are also powerful ways of bringing the body into balance.

3. Craniosacral therapy
Studying and receiving Biodynamic cranial osteopathy taught me to listen to what the body, mind and soul needed. I learned to surrender to the Breath of Life and trust that it reveals an inherent treatment plan that allows structure and psyche to come into alignment with his or her true Essence.

4. Acupuncture and energetic healing
Acupuncture, Jin Shin Do, Jin Shin Jyutsu, Reiki, Polarity and Therapeutic touch helped me to see how working with energetic fields could change my perception and bring greater peace and ease.

5. Healthy living habits
Nutrition and exercise.

Many books have been written on nutrition, and sometimes it takes time, experimentation, assistance from a skilled professional, and engaging our intuition to find out what best suits our individual biochemical uniqueness.

Exercise is also a vast topic and can include yoga, martial arts, chi gong, tai, chi, aerobics, weight lifting, swimming, golfing, hiking and many others. Again, it's important to find what is best attuned to us as individuals. We must find a modality that feels healing and doesn't injure us.

6. Psychological therapies
When my marriage became strained and I realized that having a successful practice and all the material things I wanted didn't bring happiness, I started doing therapy: Gestalt, Transactional Analysis, Reichian work. I saw that I was conditioned by my past and there were many historical imprints that were stored in my unconscious and body. These imprints or impressions often controlled my behavior and contributed to my unhappiness. They limited my experiences and perceptions. Bringing unconscious impressions and imprints on my soul to the light of consciousness helped me become lighter, happier and more flexible.

7. Somatic Psychology, including Bodynamics Integration, Hakomi and Somatic Experiencing
After five years of practice I began to see how profoundly emotions and beliefs affected physical structure, physiology and chemistry. I enrolled in a Masters program in psychological counseling. I began to study somatic psychology, which taught me how patterns in our body, mind and physiology influence our state. The way we stand, sit, move and make gestures expresses how we see and perceive our world.

8. Expressive therapies

Art, music, poetry, writing and dance have powerful ways of healing our body and psyche. Doing art over many years has changed my view of life and the world and transformed many of the habitual concepts I had about seeing.

Being immersed in the world of shape, design, composition and value influenced the way I shaped, designed, valued and put my life together. Line, rhythm and color helped me notice different shades and subtleties of feeling and emotion.

9. A spiritual path

The Diamond Approach has been my spiritual path for the last 27 years. It encourages students to become full human beings in the world, involved in regular everyday activities while grounded in the eternal spirit.

This teaching helps us to be mindful, practice meditation, inquire and engage awareness.

Gifted professionals, teachers, loved ones, and spiritual friends have supported me in becoming more mindful and encouraged me stay in present awareness and explore my experience. By becoming aware of and accepting what arises in the moment, I was able to gain understanding, clarity, wisdom, and insight. Being present and aware helped me to metabolize my day-to-day experiences and move toward wholeness. My perspective changed. New options arose. My life became fuller, happier and more fulfilling.

10. ANGELS

Friends, relatives, therapists, skilled professionals and other angels who lent a helping hand.

11. Nature and pets

Last but not least, trees, flowers, mountains, the ocean, dogs, cats, birds, salamanders, fish, chickens, turtles – whatever lifts your spirit and brings you pleasure.

My wish is that you will be touched by the poems in this little book. If you haven't already done so, may you find your own unique path to transformation and healing.

15	Precious Child

BEGINNINGS

19	I Will Be Born
21	Struggle
23	Vanishing Twin
25	My Mother
29	Mother and Child Portrait
31	I Wake Up Screaming
33	I Was a Good Girl
37	It's My Fourth Birthday
39	Terror at Age Five
43	Precious Child
45	Broken Nose
49	Like Waves in the Ocean

THE HOUSE

55	This Old House
57	House of My Father
59	Grandma's House

ALLIES

63	Gibby
71	Ode to My Grandmother
77	Beloved Uncle Pie
83	Earth Mother (for Hannah)
85	Hannah Ostergaard

MOTHER AND FATHER

89	When I Look Deeper
91	Powerless in the Face of Death
93	Mourning
95	Mother dying
105	Daddy
107	My Father at 95
109	Bright Sunny Day
113	Dad's Funeral

WE STAND

117	I Learned That
119	Pink Alamanda
121	Grace
123	Joy
127	Rainbow Drops
129	Whose Life Am I Living Anyway?
131	Yesterday, Today and Now
133	Cypress Tree
135	Waves of Change (from Hokusai's Wave)
137	Katharine Stone Ayers
139	I Was Born to
141	Golden dusk
143	Silent Reminiscing

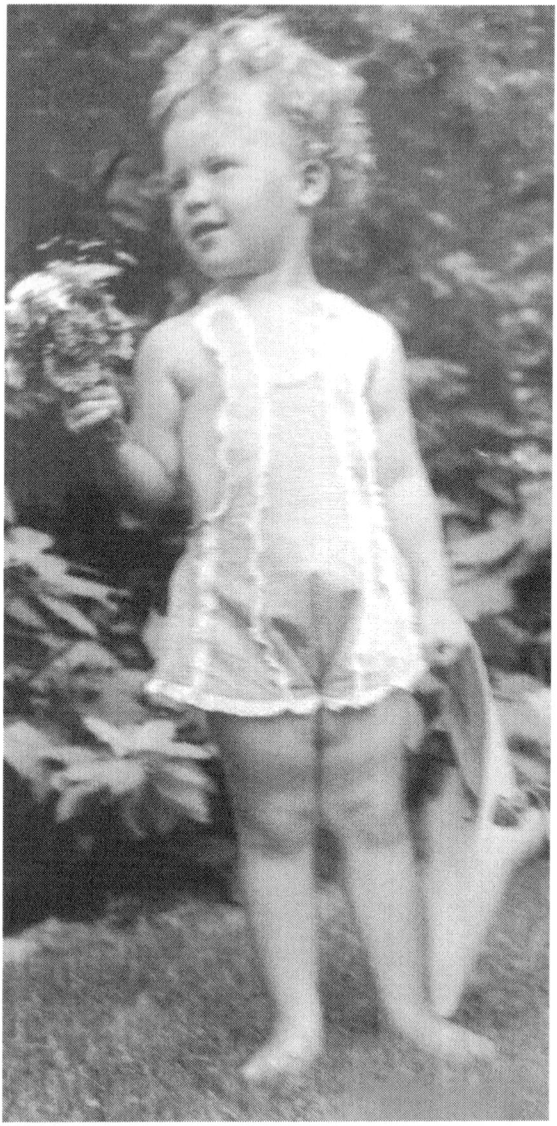

PRECIOUS CHILD

O child of beauty and grace
I hold your preciousness as a lantern
your light illuminates my way
consoles me
May you always shine so brightly

BEGINNINGS

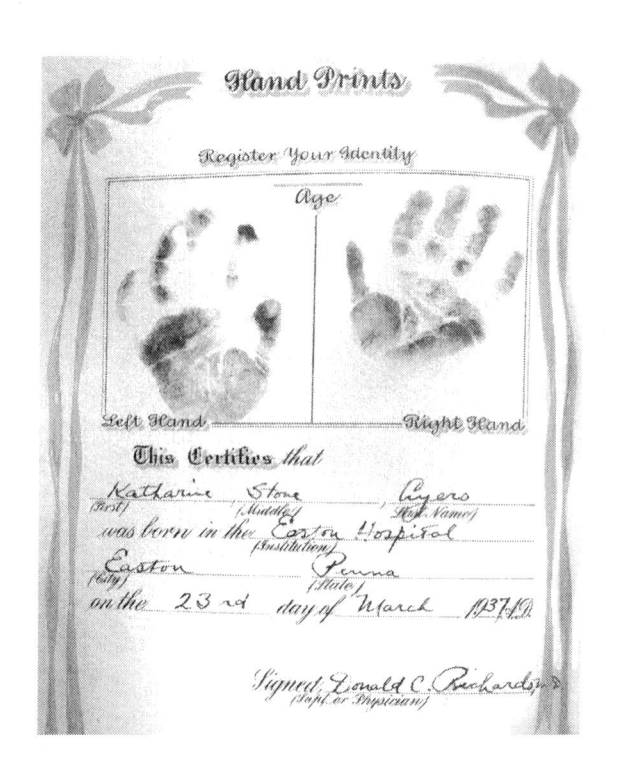

Hand Prints

Register Your Identity

Age

Left Hand   *Right Hand*

This Certifies that

Katharine (First), Stone (Middle), Ayers (Last Name)

was born in the Easton Hospital (Institution)

Easton (City), Penna (State)

on the 23rd day of March 1937 A.D.

Signed, Donald C. Richardson M.D. (Supt. or Physician)

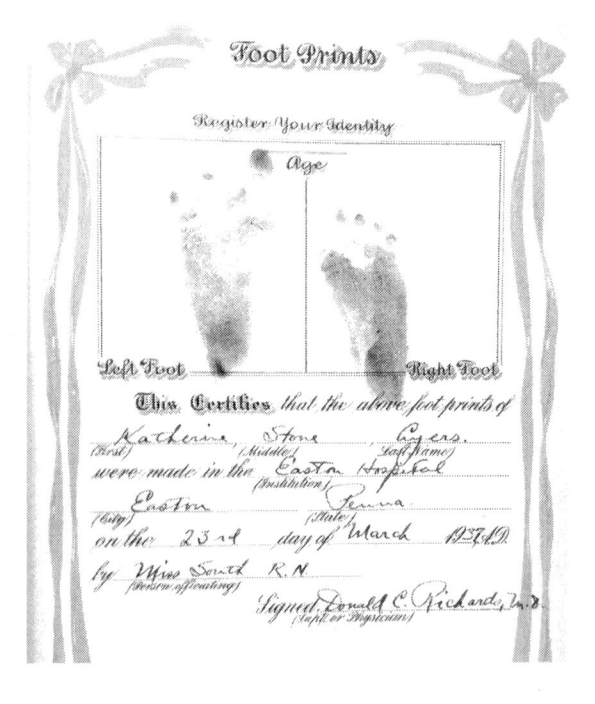

Foot Prints

Register Your Identity

Age

Left Foot   *Right Foot*

This Certifies that the above foot prints of

Katharine (First), Stone (Middle), Ayers (Last Name)

were made in the Easton Hospital (Institution)

Easton (City), Penna (State)

on the 23rd day of March 1937 A.D.

by Miss South R.N. (Person officiating)

Signed, Donald C. Richardson M.D. (Supt. or Physician)

I WILL BE BORN

tomorrow to a woman
who will be scared.
The Doctor will give her three kinds of anesthesia
and a spinal to calm her taut nerves.

I will enter the world prematurely,
drugged, half comatose,
choked with the umbilical cord around my neck,
dragged out by forceps,
whisked away to a nursery.

I will wish that I could go back to the angels.

Struggle will arise inside me,
knowing that I am stuck between two worlds.

This woman will be depressed for months,
unable to hold or bond with me.
I will be filled with longing for loving connection
for the rest of my life.

STRUGGLE

I'm moving down a Fallopian tube. No place to land. A hostile uterus…like a garbage dump. My mother's terror, smoking, drinking?

Struggle to implant. Struggle to thrive in the womb. Struggle to be born. Struggle.

VANISHING TWIN

When a friend finishes giving me a craniosacral session he says, "How was that for you?"

I'm reluctant to tell him what happened, but decide to go ahead.

I'm a fetus in the stage of looking like a sea horse with gigantic eyes. My twin is beside me. His eyes are gigantic too. We're looking at each other. He is not happy about being in a toxic uterus, an environment flooded with our mother's anger, fear and terror. Being born into a very dysfunctional family feels like too much. His life force begins to wane. *Oh my God, my buddy is leaving! I want to hold on to him. I can't do this alone. It's too tough trying to survive in this crazy environment.*

He keeps dissolving. Rotting in the womb. I'm bereft, despairing.

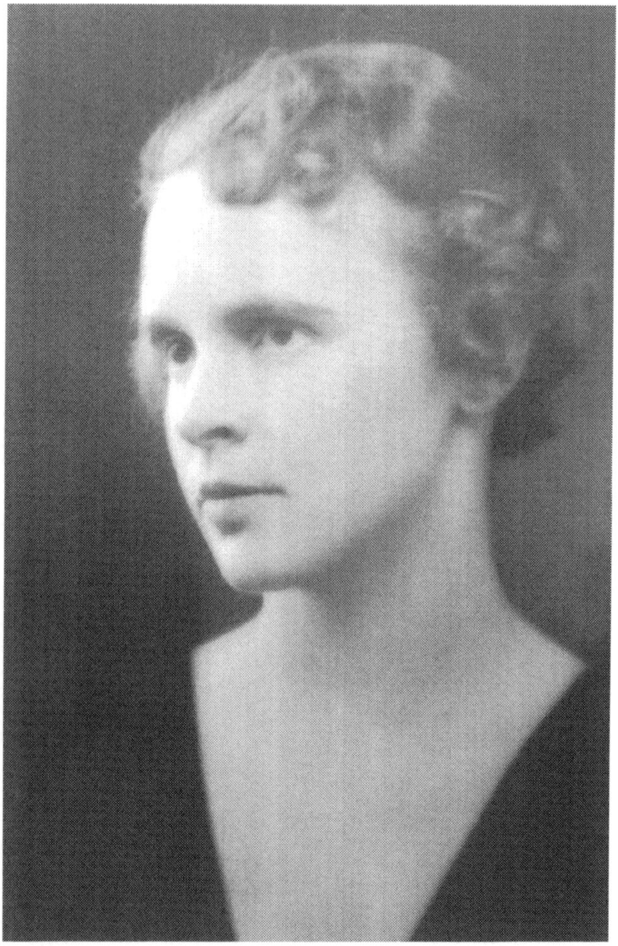

Katharine Stone Ayers

MY MOTHER

I asked my mother about her pregnancy, my birth and our early life together. She said *"Don't ever ask me anything like that again. I would never have asked my mother such questions."*

Then…*"The vertigo to announce that you were on your way was traumatic. I went upstairs to the bathroom and threw up. Then I was taken to the hospital and put on sugar IV's."*

When she told my Dad she was pregnant he reacted with anger and disbelief. "We can't afford to have a child."

I asked her if her pregnancy was pleasant. *"Not really… as I look back there wasn't really a happy anticipation preparing for what should have been a joyous and happy event. All very matter of fact."*

The day I was born my Dad didn't show up at the birth. Later he brought his mother and brother Larry to the hospital. My mother despised them both. *"I was hurt. No loving embrace – No baby on my belly. You were in the room where all the babies were kept. Joe saw you through the window. All very sterile. I was in the hospital three weeks. That was routine in those days. How cruel, really, when we both needed each other."*

I wept as she spoke of our lack of bonding and connection.

My mother said she was sick and depressed after I was born. My birth certificate says the Doctor gave her four kinds of anesthesia: a spinal, nitrous oxide, ether and sodium pentothal.

"The doctor recommended his 'best nurse' so she could 'keep you clean'. She did – and fed you your formula on time." My mother called her a 'horrible person who didn't like babies." Why did she hire her?

"I didn't have enough milk, was very depressed. I used to stay awake at night worrying that I couldn't take care of you. I was afraid that I would drop you, or that you would smother to death in your crib. I scarcely touched you."

I was shocked. Awful to hear about severe deprivation and how I was immersed in a sea of my Mother's fears and worries. Fears and worries I thought were mine.

"The nurse came home with me for three months. I was treated like an invalid. She took complete charge. She was tall, thin, not young, always in uniform. She seldom smiled. She ate with us. I had a girl who cooked, and the nurse was treated like a favored guest. Joe detested her. Since my milk supply was poor, you were given supplementary bottle feedings… By the time the nurse left, we must have been complete strangers… and I had worked myself into a full-blown case of stage fright. As I look back, I realize how much you probably needed me and how ridiculous not to enjoy every precious minute I could have with you."

Lifelong feelings of longing, aching loneliness, a haunting sense that no one was there.

Mother and Me pastel portrait by Wilbur Fiske Noyes

Katharine Stone Ayers

MOTHER AND CHILD PORTRAIT

My mother smiles a half-hearted smile.
as she poses for a pastel portrait.

It's important to look good.

Mom holds me in her arms.
Her attention is somewhere else.

Is there any connection between us?

I look bloated and disorientated
even though the artist portrays me
in alluring pastel colors.

What is going on in my baby soul?

The portrait is over seventy years old now.
Soft pastel dust is stuck on the glass.
My mother's face has become blemished.

Time has eroded her pretty façade.

I WAKE UP SCREAMING

I wake up screaming. Mom rushes into my bedroom. *"I've had a bad dream Mom!"* I say breathlessly pulling the covers tightly over me.

"It's just a dream. Go back to sleep." she says dismissively.

If it's just a dream, then why is my heart pounding, why am I so scared? Mom tucks me in, moves towards the door. I want her to stay, but she seems impatient to go back to bed. She hurries toward the door, pulls it shut behind her.

Alone in the dark, I curl up in a ball under the covers. I'm four years old. My body is shaking. Images from my dream keep running through my head. They play over and over.

I see a dead man at the bottom of a slimy green pond. I feel compassion for him. I dive down to the bottom of the pond and drag him from the water. His body is slimy and rubbery. It feels yucky. I have a silver spoon, fill it with water and mud. I feed him. He awakens in a fury, jumps up, chases me. I run like crazy because I think he wants to kill me. I wake up screaming.

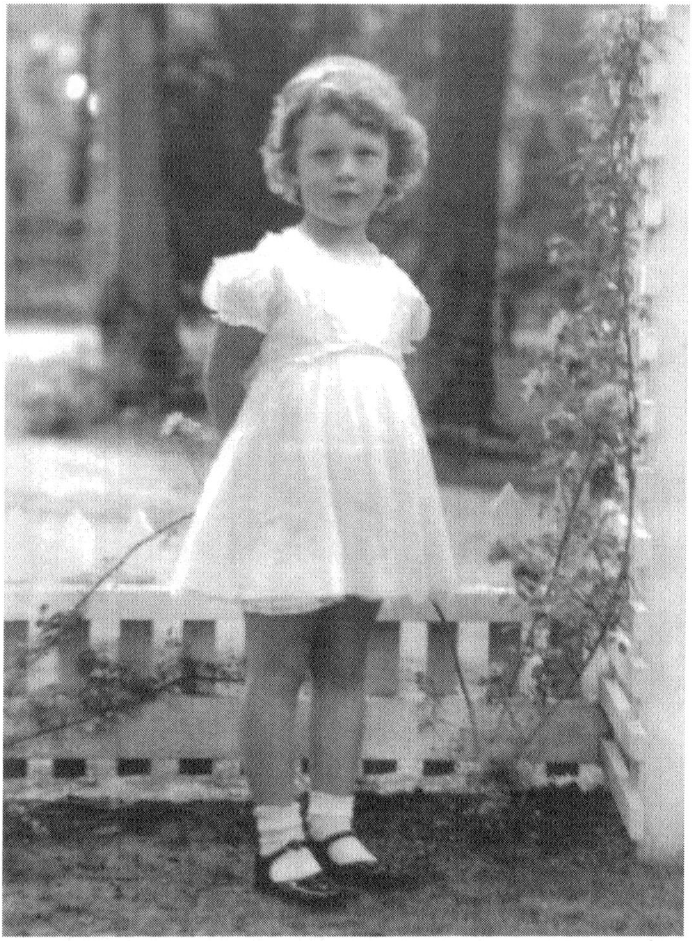

Katharine Stone Ayers

I WAS A GOOD GIRL

At cocktail hour I curtsied
for Mom and Dad's jeweled stale perfumed, powdered ladies
and starched collared, raucous off-color joking men.

I made my bed,
cleaned up my room,
did my homework,
obeyed my teachers.

Tried, tried, tried to please everybody
Pushed, pushed, pushed to do it right.

Why haven't I found love?

Got a degree in art,
studied the masters,
made dozens of flower, landscape and portrait paintings
in oil, watercolor, pastel,
charcoal sketches
of young , old faces
curvaceous bodies.

Does anyone appreciate me?

Studied hard,
became a doctor
stayed long hours into the night
for ailing patients
gave them extra time and attention.

Is anyone going to be attuned to me?

Old Remnants – New Buds

Studied psychology,
wanted to understand what made people tick
supported and empowered my clients.

Who will support and empower me?

Joined spiritual groups
meditated almost everyday for twenty-five years.
learned to sense, look and listen,
be present and aware.

Why haven' t I found peace?

Last night I had a disturbing dream,
couldn't pull it together
I was a young girl trying to pack and get ready
to go to San Francisco,
missed my bus connection to the airport,
I went crying to Mom to help me,
she said, "I won't support you-
you don't trust me."

When I woke up it felt like someone
ripped my guts out.
Utterly alone, bereft,
helpless, hopeless, despairing.

Will I ever be happy?

I cried and cried and cried,
felt lighter, saner.

Katharine Stone Ayers

As I wiped away the tears,
an exquisite Presence filled me
with gentle support,
deep bottomless caring,
quiet joy,
soft vast spacious love

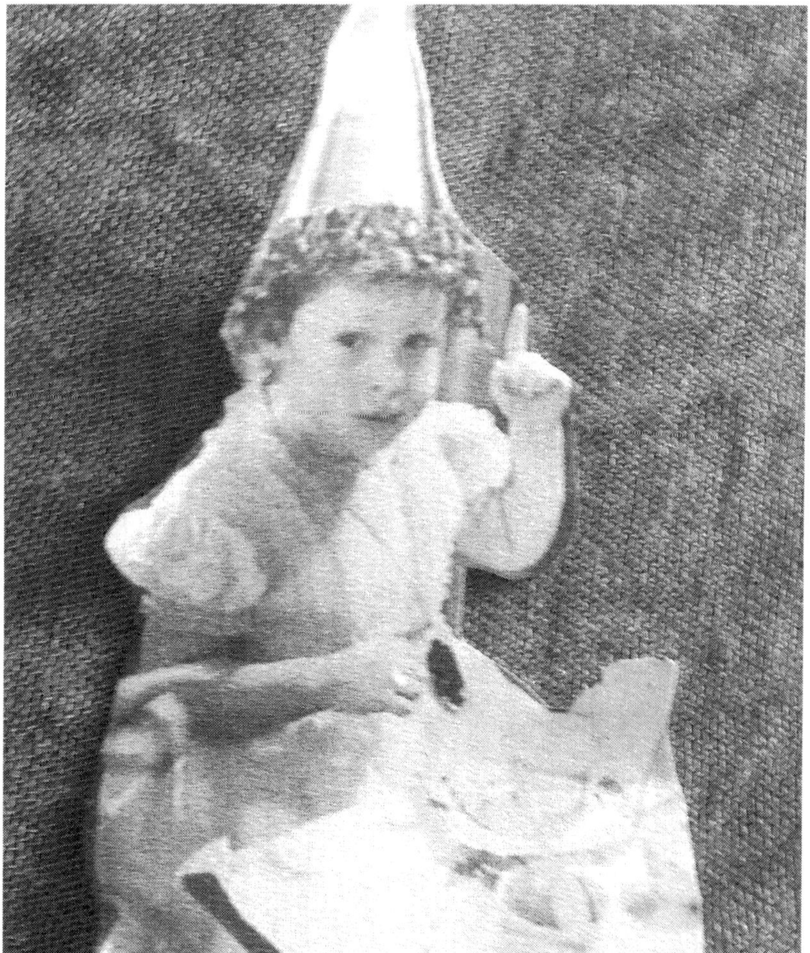

Katharine Stone Ayers

IT'S MY FOURTH BIRTHDAY

Who are all these little boys and girls Mom and Dad invited?

Sons and daughters of rich, important people?

Daddy stands on a chair with his flash camera. "Smile!"

I don't want to smile. I fake it.

We sit on tiny chairs wearing pointed little silver hats with tassels blowing paper birthday horns and whistles.

Mom says "Come on upstairs to my bedroom. I have a surprise!

A cartoon movie."

"Mom, can I collect the tickets outside your door? I say excitedly.

"You're too young," she snaps.

"It's my birthday. Why can't I?"

Mom turns and asks Susan Morrison who is about two years older.

I'm angry and jealous. I barely notice the movie. Waves of rage and heat move up my body as Bugs Bunny and Donald Duck flash on the screen.

I'm disappointed, ashamed that I'm angry.

It's my birthday.

Shock and Terror tempera painting
by Katharine Stone Ayers

Katharine Stone Ayers

TERROR AT AGE FIVE

How did a centipede bring up a terrifying memory from my unconscious?

I tell Marianne that I turned over in my bed to turn on the light in the middle of the night, felt a strong penetrating electrical shock on the back of my neck. To my horror I watched a foot long centipede race across my pillow.

Marianne notices that my body is collapsing to the right and moves her body next to me, gives me support. Comforting not to have to hold myself up. I begin to relax. Frightening surreal images and memories surface.

Marianne says to sense my body, let the images and sensations flow. Cold shivers start traveling up my arms. My teeth chatter. Terror grips me. Every part of my body is fiercely trying to hold on.

"Just let the memories surface," Marianne said calmly.

I question the reality of the images and memories. We lived in a safe neighborhood, how could this have happened? Marianne asks me to say, *"It never happened."* Everything becomes surreal again. I feel disembodied. Marianne asks me to say, *"What happened a long time ago was real."* My body begins to shake. I hyperventilate again. As the images, feelings and sensations become more vivid, I realize I hadn't made up a story.

My mind wants to deny that trauma happened, but my body remembers.

I'm five. It's late afternoon, early evening. While Grandma's helper, Barna, prepares supper I decide to go on an adventure.

My heart pounds with excitement under my little blue print dress as I decide to go for an evening walk. The sun casts long purple shadows over the sandy furrows in my grandmother's driveway. I'm exuberant, proud to be going out on my own. As I start to walk along the quiet country road, I notice a gaunt looking man with dark hair wearing blue coveralls standing in the woods just back from the roadside. He carries a bunny and motions to me. The bunny looks so cute, soft and cuddly that I go to him. The skinny man grabs me by the wrist swings me fast and wildly in big circles. I fall to the ground dizzy, disoriented. I pass out. Pain wakes me up when he starts sticking sticks up my vagina and rectum. I struggle, but realize I've been tied down. He says he will slit the bunny's throat and kill me if I tell. As he unties me and leaves, he kicks me in the left side of my rib cage.

"Strange," I told Marianne, *"this was the exact place in my chest where I had pain when my left lung collapsed from an abscess in 1983, some forty years later."* I also had drainage tubes on this side of my chest after the abscess was surgically removed.

I stand bewildered in the woods thinking about what I'll tell Barna. I stagger home. When Barna asks me, I tell her, *"I fell on a blueberry bush,"* hoping that she would believe me. Barna takes me upstairs and puts me in the shower. I'm bleeding, hurting, ashamed. She hands me a cup of tea with lemon and honey as she tucks me into bed. She sits on the side of my bed for a long time. (Perhaps she suspects something.) I long to tell her what happened, but have a sinister feeling that the crazy man might find out, come and kill me. I don't want Barna to leave, but am unable to ask her to stay. I feel as though I'd caused enough trouble for the day. Barna turns off the light and heads downstairs. The room feels so dark. I turn on my side clutch my pillow and contract into a little ball trying to ease the emptiness, aching loneliness, deep grief in my heart. Nighttime never felt so long, sad and lonely.

At the end of my session with Marianne, we talk softly for a while. An enormous burden was lifted out of my body. My body continues to relax and an exquisite sense freedom rushs through my veins. An internal heaviness that had plagued me for most of my life starts to melt. Lightness remains.

After a long pause, Marianne looks thoughtful as she explains, *"It's my experience that difficult to diagnose malignancies are frequently linked to trauma that had to be kept secret."* I feel strangely relieved, but also sad about the toll that keeping this trauma secret had had on my body.

We were both quiet for a while. Then Marianne looks at me with love and compassion and says, *"I think we have taken the fangs off the serpent that created your leukemia."*

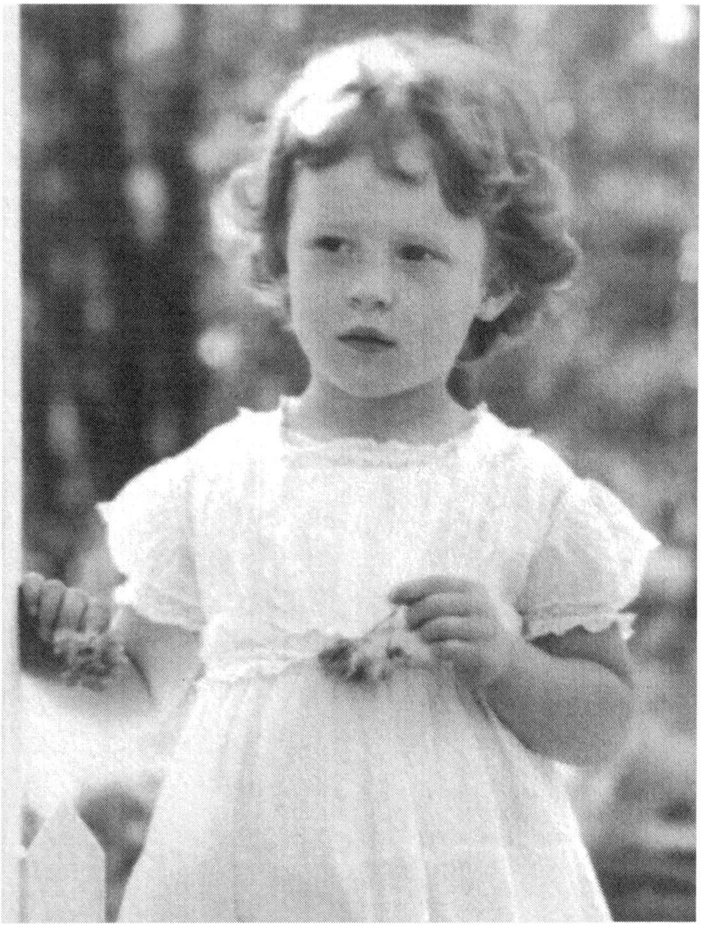

PRECIOUS CHILD

Precious child,
orphan,
hovering on the edge of darkness.

Darkness
hides
an inner glow,
covers love and creativity.

Little one,
your burning core
has not yet melted
your shell of insecurity.

Silently, cautiously
a spark moves through you
creating greater opening and grace.

Startle painting by Katharine Stone Ayers

BROKEN NOSE

Mom's in a snit, complains that Daddy is late for dinner again, insists that we have to wait for him even though the food is getting cold.

It seems like hours later when he finally bursts into the kitchen, weaves into the dining room with a stupid grin on his face, chuckles to himself, smelling of beer and peanuts.

"Hello," he says teetering, looking like he expects us to share his drunken glee.

"Hello," I mumble under my breath trying to conceal my anger. His body lunges towards me, his fist explodes into my nose with a loud crack, blood streams down my face. I run up the stairs, head for the bathroom where I can lock the door behind me. He catches up with me on the stairs, grabs my right arm, wrenches it behind my back screaming, *"You say hello to me when I talk to you!"*

My arm feels like it is being twisted out of its socket. I scream back, *"Hello, hello, hello, hello..."* as I break away from him, run, lock the bathroom door behind me. I'm shaking. Blood is spilling on the tiny black and white tiles on the bathroom floor.

Our Nanny knocks desperately on the door over and over, pleading with me to let her in. Thinking she might know how to stop the bleeding or can help me, I unlock the door. She draws water into the tub. I climb in, the water turns pink. The Nanny moves towards me. I feel rage and shock surging through my body as I throw buckets of bloody water at her with super human strength screaming, *"Get out! Get away from me!"*

I hear Mom yelling at Dad, *"You get in there and apologize to your daughter."*

He's the last person I want to see. I cringe when I see him standing in the bathroom door. Unconvincingly he says, *"I'm sorry."*

Nude and ashamed, I watch him as he impatiently anticipates my answer. I hesitate, fearing he'll hit me again if I say how terrorized and angry I am.

"That's OK," knowing in every fiber in my being that I don't mean it. Something inside collapses knowing I've betrayed myself to stay safe.

Like Waves in the Ocean pastel painting by Katharine Stone Ayers

LIKE WAVES IN THE OCEAN

Each breath
expand and contract

Ups and downs,
like the waves in the ocean,
hills and valleys,

Inhale –
Painting coy swimming,
drawing the human figure,
I open, focus, become clearer.

Exhale –
Tenth grade in an
uptight upstate New York boarding school
my stomach contracts into a tight little ball
my breathing gets shallow.

Inhale –
When I'm with you,
my heart, eyes, ears open
to receive you.

Exhale –
You hurl harsh words at me,
my ears shut down,
my vision gets blurry
I lose my contact with my center.

Inhale –
I walk my dog, Rosie on the beach
pick roses,
swim in the ocean,
my body relaxes.
Joy arises.

Exhale –
My parents fight at the dinner table,
my hands clench,
my forearms and head
get tight.

When I connect
with the parts of me that are tight, contracted,
they open and expand,
become lighter.

Inhale – exhale
When I dance,
my feet touch the earth
feel the rhythm
of music,
connect to God.

THE HOUSE

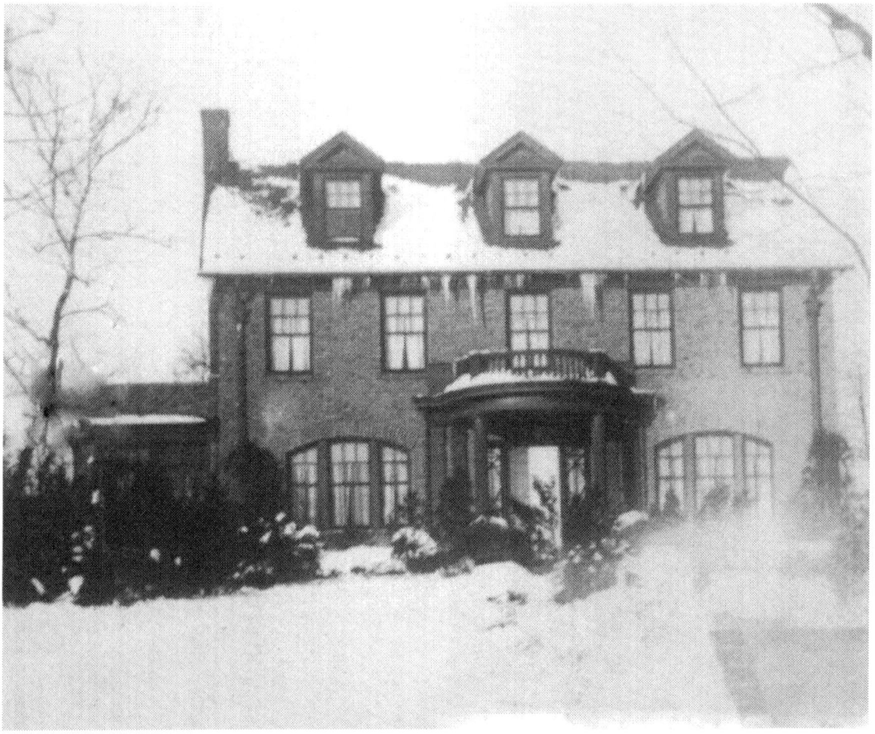

Katharine Stone Ayers

THIS OLD HOUSE

My sister told me she had a dream –
our childhood home was dark,
there was nothing she wanted from inside,
except the dog.

No one from the outside guessed how dark.

The exterior looked solid
yellow ochre bricks,
long cement walk way.
porch over a sturdy front door.
A grassy expanse and willowy birch tree in the front yard,
a huge mulberry and maple to climb in the backyard.

No one knew about the chaos inside:

Doors slamming, rage, screaming, name calling,
physical and mental violence.

My bed on the third floor was next to a storage closet
that housed an old skull that Daddy called "Yorick."
Freaked me out.

No one knew.

A crystal chandelier
hung over a mahogany dining room table with fine china and
sterling silverware.

Old Remnants – New Buds

Chippendale chairs in the living room with satin covers.
Polite dinner parties.

It didn't make up for Daddy's drinking, nasty remarks, fights at cocktail hour.

I found ways to be away from home:
pajama parties with friends,
playing baseball with the boys after school,
bike riding to another town.

It was a dreary house.

HOUSE OF MY FATHER

I don't want to live in the house of my father:
insist that everyone conform to my point of view,
argue like my life depended on it,
work long hours at home and office,
medicate myself at the end of the day with a dry martini.

Booze doesn't ease my pain.
I just feel like shit the next day.
Pushing and shoving, trying to make things happen.
Accomplishing can create a temporary euphoria
then it disappears into depression and fatigue.

I don't want to live in the house of my father.

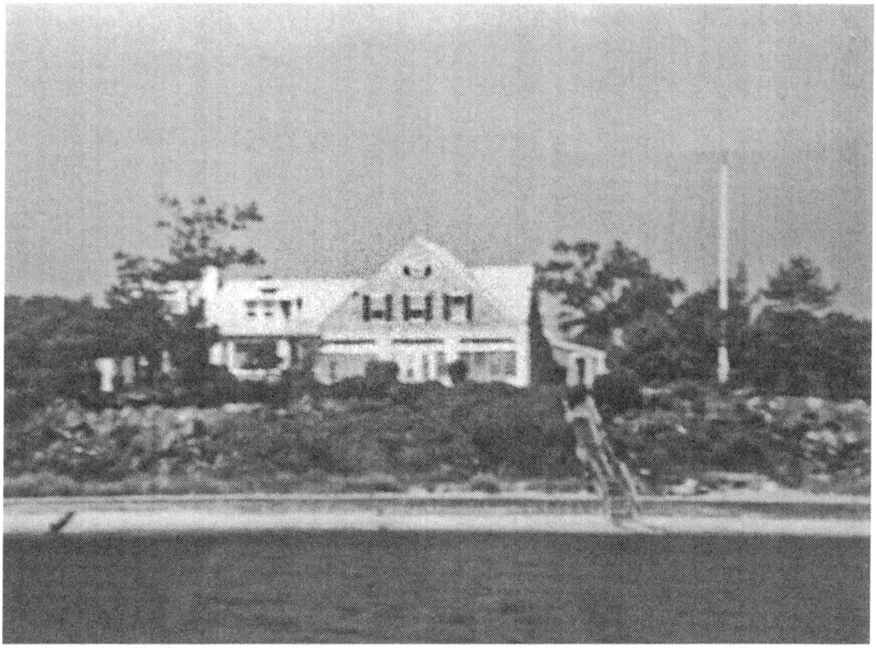

GRANDMA'S HOUSE

My bare feet sink into a soft blanket of pine needles along the sandy path to Grandma's house. Pine scents and salt-spray aromas fill the air. West Bay stretches blue beyond the sand cliffs. My heart expands. I feel fresh and alive. I'm grateful for Grandma, the ocean, the pine forest.

Dew is fresh on the morning glories adorning the white picket fence behind the back porch of her home. Rainbow droplets shimmer in the warmth of the morning sun. I move my head in all directions and see bursts of orange, blue and icy clear green that emanate from raindrops. Joy and delight! Elegant blue purple radiance hangs in the morning stillness.

As the sun climbs higher, hydrangeas emerge out the shadows along the driveway. Flowers within flowers touch each other, delicate pinks, lavenders, blue bell blue, deep ocean blue and purples. I wander through Grandma's rose garden sniffing deep red, pink, yellow, white and lavender roses.

I make my way to the back door where I meet Grandpa wearing his brown crinkly paper slippers and a rubber-bathing hat rolled over his ears. His flat feet head towards the grey weathered wooden stairs that lead to a long wooden pier with a driving board on the end. He stands with his back to the water. He bends his knees springs upwards, arches his back and does a perfect back dive.

I can do that! I say to myself. I go to the end of the board. I want to show off for Grandpa. I fly backwards. SLAP! I land with my back flat on the water. I hold back the tears. While I wait for the sting to go away, I see that Grandpa didn't even notice. Or maybe, he pretended not to see. So much for trying to impress Grandpa.

I hose off and enter the back porch. The screen door slams behind me. Barna, my Grandmother's maid, is busy in the kitchen. She offers me a cup of tea. Her long red hair touched with grey is braided in loops around her head. She is slender and has a calm, graceful manner. We don't speak of our affection for one another, but my heart feels warm and safe in her presence. When I was little, she made me bowls of oatmeal. I put heaps of sugar or honey, or both on top, and she let me. It was wartime; sugar and honey were rationed.

A sign in Grandma' dining room said, "Use less sugar and stir like hell."

My heart expands. I feel fresh and alive. I'm grateful for Grandma, the ocean, the pine forest.

ALLIES

Gibby and Me

Katharine Stone Ayers

GIBBY

Norman Rockwell did a painting for Post magazine that I couldn't get out of my mind, a cuddly black and white Cocker Spaniel with the big soulful eyes. She looked so vulnerable and decorative with her black back and white underbelly and the interesting pattern of black dots on her paws. When I was ten, I begged and pestered my Mother to get me a black and white cocker spaniel, like the one on the Post magazine, until one day she said, *"Cousin Tillie wrote and said that has a neighbor who has a dog just like the one you saw on the magazine."*

"Oh boy!" I exclaimed, *"Can we go and pick her up?*

"I've made arrangements for Spring break," she said. When that happy day arrived, my younger sister, Phyllis and I piled into the back seat of our Mercury, Mom headed from our home in Pennsylvania to Maryland and Aunt Tillie's farm, which she called Green Bough. My sister was grumpy most of the trip. I asked her, *"What's going on Phyl?"* I got the silent treatment, which was often her MO when she was upset, which left me to fantasize what might be going on in her mind. Was she bothered because we weren't going to fetch her a dog, and that it was going to be my dog. She hadn't shown any interest in having a dog. My Mother tried to placate Phyl, saying, *"Just think of how much fun it'll be to be on a farm. You always wanted to live in the country."* My sister wasn't buying it. She sat in the back seat and pouted.

Old Remnants – New Buds

Aunt Tillie, a portly woman with flaming red hair and an earthy voice, met us at her front door that evening. It was dinnertime and she prepared a stew of vegetables from her garden and chicken from her farm. *"We'll go to my neighbor's, Sally's house, tomorrow morning to pick up your puppy,"* she said as she wished us goodnight. The night was silent, except for a train that passed by nearby, clacking and penetrating the inky blackness, and roosters that crowed persistently before dawn. I was so excited that I didn't sleep much. We were greeted with fresh eggs and bacon in the morning. I listened impatiently as Aunt Tillie told Mom about the hardships and hard work of farm life. Aunt Tillie's husband died the year before, leaving her even more exhausted by the sheer enormity of daily chores. Finally, we took off to see Sally.

Sally came out with my puppy in her arms, and it was love at first sight.

A darling, fluffy little bundle of affection! Sally carefully handed her to me and she melted like a beanbag into my arms. I was in heaven, and spent the ride back home holding her and petting her silky hair, the full length of her back and belly, as she molded herself into a soft ball in my lap. *"What are you going to name her?"* Mom asked.

I thought for a long moment and said. *"GB, Gibby for Green Bough."*

My Dad was less than thrilled with my new canine companion. When he entered the room with his usual overbearing and brusque demeanor, she cowered and pied on the Persian rug in the living room. *"Damn, stupid dog,"* he muttered. I felt sad and protective of Gibby and could relate to her reaction. I often cowered inside and felt afraid of Dad. Dad had a formidable presence and a hot temper. Gibby must have picked up on it. Besides, my Dad didn't like women, including his Mom. I often heard him make slurring remarks like, *"Just like a damn female."* One day he introduced me to a husband and wife team, two PhD chemists, and told me afterwards, *"She is the brains of the outfit, but she is smart enough not to let anyone know it."* Now he was surrounded by four ladies, Mom, Phyl, Gibby and me.

I suspect that my Dad took refuge in his dog, Penny, a copper colored Cocker Spaniel, who, like him, was an independent, adventurous, macho and outgoing type. Dad traveled a lot. He claimed that it was for his business, but in his later years he admitted that he also needed a break from Mom. They fought a lot. Their yelling and slamming of doors scared me. In later life, and after many therapy sessions, I understood how terrifying it was for my sister and I to be in an environment where our parents acted like three year olds. We coped by telling each other jokes, amusing ourselves with burping contests, overeating, butter, ice cream and macaroni and cheese.

Whenever my Dad left town, his dog, Penny, would disappear for days. Friends would tell us stories about seeing Penny in neighboring towns, some fifteen, twenty miles away. Penny always showed up on the day that my Dad returned home and greeted him exuberantly, barking, licking, tail-wagging. My Dad valued loyalty, and Penny gave it to him.

Gibby had a different temperament than Penny altogether. She was gentle, yielding, sensitive and a malleable little creature. One day we dressed her up in a frilly baby's cap and a white lacey dress, and propped her up in a living room chair with her black and white paw on the armrest. She leaned comfortably into the chair and stayed put. Moments later, one of my Mother's maudlin friends, who came to visit, entered the living room, exclaiming. *"Oh my, what a darling BAB..."* The last letter of baby trailed off into silence as her jaw dropped and her face went flat and ashen. My sister and I held our hands over our mouths trying to suppress our giggles.

Old Remnants – New Buds

I felt sad to leave Gibby behind when I left for boarding school. I'd get to see her on summer vacations, Christmas and Easter and on an occasional weekend, but I had my doubts about leaving her at home. I'd seen Gibby's little body crumple when my Mother was cooking in the kitchen and yelled, *"Get out of my way!"* as she kicked my precious companion. Gibby would slink away stunned with an incomprehensible look in her sad eyes. My mother was a nervous and fearful woman and didn't like anyone impinging on her space.

One day I asked her, *"Mom, what are you afraid of?"*

"Everything." she said much to my astonishment. That must be awful, I thought to myself, with a vague sense of powerlessness, knowing that I probably couldn't do anything about it, even though I tried.

One late afternoon my sister asked *"Can I take Gibby for a walk?"*

"As long as you put her on a leash," I replied. The main street through town was half a block from our house and had a steady stream of cars and big trucks. After she left, I worried and a wave of distrust and concern passed through my body, as I remembered my sister's stubborn streak and how she usually wanted to do things her way.

An hour later, Phyllis showed up at the front door with an agonized look on her face, tears streaming down her cheeks. *"Are you OK?"* I asked, sensing that something is terribly wrong and imagining the worst. Gibby was nowhere in sight.

"Yes."

"Thank God," I said, meaning thank God that you are Ok. I really wanted to say, *"What have you done with my dog?"*

And at the same time as I said, *"Thank God,"* she said, *"Gibby's been run over."* When she heard me say thank God, she shrieked and went screaming into the dining room into the arms of my mother. I didn't understand her reaction.

Something in my belly sank, and my mind went on hyper alert with unanswered questions and wondering what I could do. *Oh no! Is Gibby badly hurt? Did you kill my dog? Rage erupts inside me. Why didn't you put her on the leash? Where is she? Is she still lying in the road?*

I want to go to Gibby, comfort her, help her.

Meanwhile, my sister is crying to Mom and saying that Gibby is badly hurt and bleeding. As she wails even louder, I hear her telling Mom *"Kitty's glad that Gibby has been run over."* I can't believe my ears. What happened to make her say such a thing? Did Phyllis think that when I said *"Thank God!"* that I meant Thank God that Gibby was run over? How could she believe that I would feel that way? My darling dog, whom I love more than anything. My heart sinks. I feel betrayed.

My Mother is in a snit. Does she believe my sister's story that I'm glad that Gibby has been run over? I'm feeling really confused and disorientated. Mom grabs my sister's hand and heads for the back door. *"We're leaving to go and see Gibby, and will be back soon."*

"I want to go too," I say pleading with her.

"No, you have to stay here!"

My head is in a tailspin. *Why are they leaving me behind? Are you mad at me?* It feels cruel. *Do you believe Phyllis's story that I wanted Gibby dead?* I feel powerless, shocked and confused.

Old Remnants – New Buds

I stand in the hallway paralyzed, unable to insist that I go with them.

As my Mother slams the door behind her and the lock clicks shut, I'm caught in a vortex of grief and despair, alone in the dark with my pain and aloneness. I'm desperate to see my little angel, Gibby.

I learn later that my Mom finds a vet on the same block where a car hit Gibby. They take her from the side of the curb to his office and place her on the vet's table. As she lies there, the life drains from her precious, innocent little body.

Meanwhile. I sit at home in the dark, longing to touch and hold her one more time, mourning, missing her, not knowing if she is still alive or what do with all the mixed emotions streaming through me.

As I reflect on my past, I remember that my Mother's view was often polarized between me and my sister. She would often said, *"Why can't you be like your sister?"* (meaning why didn't I stay home and read books like my sister instead of going out to play baseball with the boys after school.) Later, I found out that she would say to my sister, *"Why can't you be more like Kitty?"* (more extraverted and enjoying exercise outdoors.) That seemed to be the norm in our family, two or three members of the family ganging up against one. I was usually the identified *"bad, rebellious one."* I remember how alienating that was and how lonely I felt, but I kept it to myself. I didn't want to give them any ammunition that would make things worse.

As I write this, I feel compassion for the little girl who was left alone and was so bereft over the lost of her dog. I feel sad that no one was there to help her process her shock and confusion. I wish I had been there to hold and comfort her, and allow her to express her feelings or say what was going on inside.

I still feel a quiet longing, wishing I could see and hold Gibby one more time, say all the words to her that were left unsaid by her sudden departure, tell her how much I love her, loved touching her and what a precious companion she was for me.

Precious companion dead
Our love bond
never dies.

Grandma Stone

Katharine Stone Ayers

ODE TO MY GRANDMOTHER

My Grandmother had long flaming red hair
rode horseback with four brothers
on a farm in Sandy Spring, Maryland.

A golf and a tennis champion, she moved
to Boston when she married my Grandfather,
supported him as a lawyer, insurance company CEO, senator,
entertained foreign dignitaries,
gave elegant dinners.

She invited me to pick roses in her rose garden,
sniffed intoxicating pink, tangerine, soft yellow, lavender aromas.
made colorful, fluffy arrangements.

Grandma loved cake, treated me
to lavish lunches with angel cake, crème Brule and cookies.

She took me to Quaker meetings
in a plain meeting hall
where no one spoke until they were inspired.
After a long silence someone stood and spoke,
golden light filled the room.

Old Remnants – New Buds

Grandma gave me a manicure
A lady never has dirt under her fingernails.
And to entice me to behave
There was a little girl who had a little curl right in the middle of her forehead. When she was good she was very, very good. When she was bad she was horrid.

When I was ill, she changed my world.
I think it's time Thee took up painting.
I began with a 3" brush and a 4" wallpaper scraper,
fascinated as lobster shacks emerged.

Grandma introduced me to her artist friend who wanted a companion. I went to the Mohave desert to live with her in the adobe home she built with her husband. I joined her classes and began to paint saguaros, desert sage and Superstition mountain.

Painting became a joy.
Years later when I moved to Big Island
I painted orchids, roses, fishermen, hula dancers.
In Maui, more flowers, lush green landscapes, aquamarine, deep blue seascapes.

Her gifts live on.

Naked Lilies photo by Katharine Stone Ayers

Katharine Stone Ayers

The scent of pink naked lady lilies in my birthday bouquet
carries me into an angelic realm sprinkled with silver sparkles
where soothing, soft harp music wafts in the breezes.

Memories of being with Grandma in her rose garden sniffing
all the multi-colored roses: yellow for joy and lemon butter,
white for purity and Tahitian vanilla, red for passion, orange
for cinnamon spice, mango nectar and ripe persimmons.

Scents and colors connect Grandma's heart and mine.

Uncle Pie at the Helm

Katharine Stone Ayers

BELOVED UNCLE PIE

Last night, at sunset, a radiant cascade of light
spread across the western sky.
I knew that you were part of that glow,
that you are okay..

How is it possible to feel so much love and sweetness
for all the warmth and caring
you have given me in my life,
and be so overcome with grief
since you left your body on Sunday?

It was hard to see
your body become weaker and more fragile.
In spite of your physical decline,
your spirit was vast, grand and strong as ever.

I cherish all the memories:
The sail to an uninhabited island
off the coast of Maine,
how we walked joyfully in the woods singing,
lay down on the warm meadow floor
with bees and the scent of grass,
drinking in midday sunshine.

Old Remnants – New Buds

I remember how safe I felt when you navigated storms at sea.

I remember screaming with delight
when you tossed us a rope and towed us behind the Sonny.
how delicious it was to be pulled faster than we could swim.

I remember humungous waves
you taught us to ride at Wellfleet,
how they massaged our bellies
as they carried us to shore.

I'll miss those nights when you read to us
by the light of kerosene lamps at Nigunak,
about Sir Richard Burton's trip to Mecca and
heartwarming stories of Littletree.

Summers at your Camp in the wilderness,
a sanctuary
where we laughed and cried together,
listened to the loons,
learned about mosses
along beautiful wooded trails you created.

Katharine Stone Ayers

At night we fed the chippies.
In the morning we'd jump into the lake, even when it was freezing
'cause who wants to hear you call us "chicken."

I'll never forget your sumptuous chocolate sauce.
You stirred the pot until it got caramelized.
I can see you licking your lips,
hear you saying
"chocolate chocolate sauce"
as you poured it over your chocolate ice cream.

I remember how we happily picked milk-bottles full of blueberries
cause you promised to cook us blueberry cake,
your enthusiasm for making fish chowder
with tarragon sauce from a fresh catch.

I can still picture you in a Yarmouth restaurant
where you and Aunt Alice used pendulums
to check out Rappe pie (mashed potatoes and gravy).
We all knew what answer you would get.

Old Remnants – New Buds

I'll even miss your teasing, pied beds and practical jokes.
Underneath all that, I never doubted your unconditional love.

I remember your laugh and smile more than anything.

In some naïve way, I thought these moments could go on forever.
and they will in my memory.

Even though I can still hear your belly laughs
remember how it was to melt into your big soft, strong hugs,
I wish I could see your smile.

Most of all I cherish
in our silent moments together
comfortable, connected.

You have given so much:
love
and joy for life.

I'm deeply grateful to know you
Thank you for the gift of being you.

I'll always love you.

Katharine Stone Ayers

Hannah and Me

EARTH MOTHER (for Hannah)

Your gentle acceptance
coaxed me tenderly
into embodiment.

You held me through dark moments–
despair, hopelessness
aching emptiness,
sublime moments
full of Presence.

You held it all.

You taught me that it is possible
to be fully alive and truthful

You showed me the beauty of connection-
that touching is natural, pleasurable,
that it is normal to be
harmonious, integrated, regulated.

I sing you,
your earthly roots
connected to the stars.

Hannah Ostergaard

Hannah your name sounds cozy, soft, makes me want to cuddle with you. Ostergaard speaks of your Danish home, but doesn't speak to your lively and passionate Jewish and gypsy ancestry. The sound of your name, Hannah, resonates through all the cells of my body, brings memories of you holding me close, telling me that you wish you were an octopus with many arms to embrace me. Hannah, my blessed earth mother. Hannah, a lyrical sound that transports me into sweet reveries. Even though you have left your earthly home, your Presence dances in the bamboo as they sway in the wind, sparkle in the rain amidst rainbows and sunlight. I taste your earthiness and the smell of you like freshly turned sod. You are the color of richness, gold brocade threaded through amber and ornate Chinese satin. You whisper gently in my ears, stories of mystical, mysterious ancient belonging to the earth, the cosmos, each other. I want to howl at the moon to bring you back again.

MOTHER AND FATHER

Young Mom and Dad

Older Mom and Dad

WHEN I LOOK DEEPER

I look into my mother's eyes,
see apathy and resignation,
fatigue, shock,
fear and hatred.

I look at my Dad's belly,
see fragility,
remnants of a shell
he tries to hold together.

Self-flagellation–
he slobbers on himself,
pokes things up his penis,
has blood stains on his underwear.
Says he got something under his skin,
scrapes his legs down to the bone,
tries to push away horrors that
threaten to arise from within.

me?
I try to distract myself
with momentary bits of pleasure:
music, nature, a beautiful home.

I hold a tiny finger
in a dam that threatens to break–
releasing a stream of depressing memories,
hopelessness, helplessness.
deprivation, rage, despair and hatred.

Anthuriums photo by Katharine Stone Ayers

POWERLESS IN THE FACE OF DEATH

I'm restless during the plane trip from Bethlehem to Hawaii, grateful to be going home. I am looking forward to my writing class with Lollie. Writing offers me an opportunity to process grief, overwhelm I feel around my Mother's dying process.

In class Lollie passes around a little box of objects to write about. I choose a dried up anthurium and a small card with a prayer on it. I write. God, grant me the serenity to accept this anthurium just as it is. I have a preference for a bright red waxy and alive anthurium that is blooming under a giant fern. I want a live flower not a dead one.

Why these preferences? Why is it hard to accept my mother's withering and drying up? It's startling and horrifying to see her eyes so desperate, her face and lips sagging. Why is her decline and decay so disturbing? Is it my own fear of failing, aging, becoming senile, incapacitated? Not being able to cope, having to be taken care of? Is it that I know there is only a shadow of a chance that there will ever be a meaningful and alive communication between us?

As she is receding, we connect even less. I'm grief stricken and powerless. Can I accept that I'm powerless to change anything? Old patterns of turmoil swirl through my head, disorient me. Can I have the wisdom to stay centered and be with myself? I pray for the courage to stay present. I want to accept her the way she is.

I'll send her lavender oil. I remember her smile when she said that she used to grow lavender.

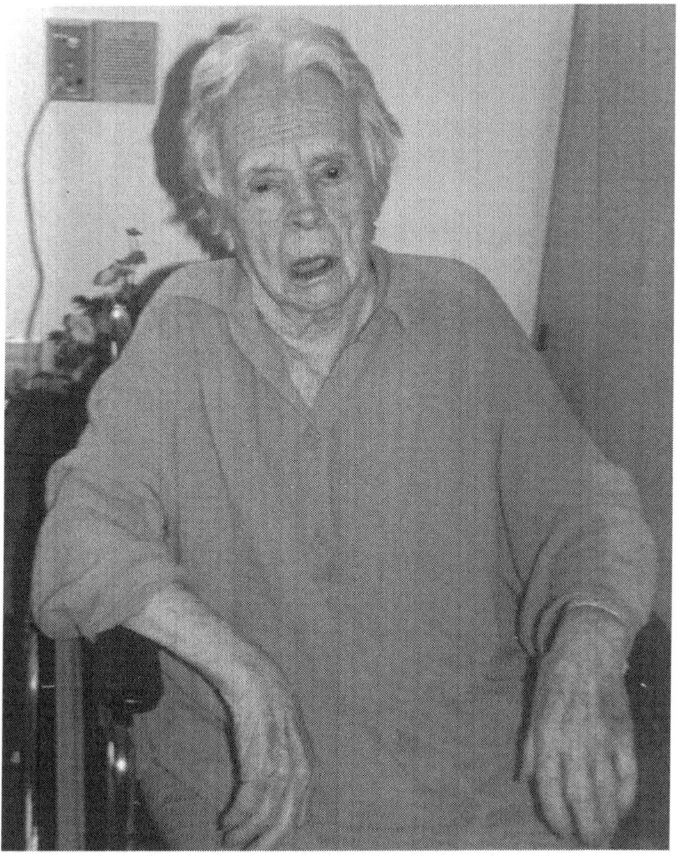

MOURNING

Mom

Your fragile, disfigured, withered body
so shrunken, contracted by fear and terror

You live in a chamber of horrors.

repeating over and over
stories about false memory syndrome,
trying to block from your memory
the law suit that my sister
filed against your pedophile husband
last vestiges
of your personality
holding on for dear life.

Joy and pleasure has flown away.

Morbidly depressed
a glimmer of something,
a fleeting moment when you connect.

I mourn you Mother,
the parts of you lost,
threw away, unfound.

My prayer for you:
May you leave misery behind,
come out from behind the walls
you've built.
Be free.
Occupy the totality
of your Being.

Katharine Stone Ayers

MOTHER DYING

The weatherman calls it an East Coast draught. It's a sticky, sultry day in Bethlehem, Pennsylvania. I feel thick and heavy inside.

Mom lies in a hospital bed at St. Luke's hospital staring off into space. A cannula hangs from her nose, her mouth droops open. Tone is gone from her face. She picks at her blankets, examines her fingers. She looks dismayed, worried, scared, despairing.

Since the last time I saw her she has broken her hip and had a stroke…according to the Doctor probably the result of a clot in her hip. My Dad claims that she lunged at him. "She attacked me!" They both fell to the ground. My Mom's hip probably snapped. She may have been reaching out for support.

The nurse raises her motorized bed so she can see me. She stares at me for a long time. I don't know if she knows that I am her daughter. Her arms and hands are shaking. I take her hand. I want to help. The shaking continues. A poignant feeling floats up and out of my chest, into my arms. I wish I could do something to soothe or comfort her.

"Carol darling," my Dad says as he tries to calm her shaking hands.

He pushes himself upright from the arms of his wheelchair, trying to stand on his emaciated legs. He places his right hand on her left shoulder, bends towards her. At age 95 his back and neck are stiff, so he reaches the rest of the way to her cheek with his lips. He gives her a soft audible smack. She shudders. I wonder what is going on in her mind.

She looks at me again. With great effort she finally speaks. "I'm so sorry."

Perhaps she means that she's sorry that she had to cancel our trip to the Poconos. "That's okay. We can do that another time..." not believing it will ever happen. Later, it occurs to me that maybe she is sorry about how mean she was to me over the years.

She fades into a sleep. My dad asks if I want to leave. I feel strangely conflicted. "It doesn't matter," I say, "I think she's tired." Inside I wish she'd wake up and I can stay and help her. I feel strangely detached, except for an occasional wave of shock, disbelief and sadness at her state of deterioration.

After a few minutes my Dad insists that we leave. I get up to go. I smooth her hair, stroke her feet. As I walk out of the hospital room, I feel pulled to go back and tell her everything will be all right. But that's my stuff. I let it go. As we exit down the hallway I feel an impulse to surround her with light and feelings of safety. So I do.

On my last visit to see my mother she is in a full time care unit at Kirkland Village. She keeps saying, "I want to go home." Perhaps she means that she wants to die. I took it to mean that she wants to go back to her apartment. Every time she pleads to be taken home, I was faced with the reality that she'll never go home again. Upstairs, above her care unit, her apartment is being dismantled. "It's policy," the Kirkland establishment says. (When a tenant can no longer care for him or herself or is no longer living in assisted care, their apartment must be vacated within 30 days.) How harsh! I can feel angry heat arising from my belly. Oh dear, I think. She's not going be able to be in her apartment ever again, surrounded by the things she loves. I want to give the management a piece of my mind for being so crass, heartless and mercenary. But, my folks had signed an agreement.

Between visits to my mother's room, I sort, allocate and give away her precious belongings. Who would benefit by having her clothes? Peggy and Dave, the Vice President of my Dad's company, decide they'll take them to Goodwill. I wonder, " Does she want someone in particular to have her silver, her china, and her antiques?" Peggy says that a friend, who lives down the hallway, wants some of her hand painted china. Mother can no longer tell us who she wants to have her possessions. It's a painful guessing game. My father's secretary, Peggy, insists, "Your mother really wants you to have those silver pieces.

I'm thinking "What in the world would I do with them in Hawaii?"

I'm distressed by the unattuned environment in my Mother's room. The patient down the hall in the special care unit yells plaintively and continuously, "Help me! Help me!" The nurses keep the TV in her room blaring all day long…one trashy program after another.

Bent on changing her room into a more healing environment, I go to the local equivalent of Long's Drug store. I buy Mom a cassette recorder, then stop by the music store to get a copy of Pachibel's Canon and some soothing classical music. When I return to my mother's room, I turn off the TV, plug in the tape recorder and play Pachibel. I ask the nurses, "My mother loves music. Would you please continue to play these tapes for her?"

Mom always loved lavender, so I put some lavender oil around her room, hang up some red, green, blue and purple fish chimes in the corner to help with the Fung Shui, and put a magnetized picture of the Dalai Lama on the wall heater next to her bed.

Old Remnants – New Buds

Visits to my mother are disconcerting. She can't talk much. I never know what she understands. Her words are slurred and almost unintelligible. Occasionally she nods when I ask her if she would like me to rub her feet. She's angry about taking her medicine and resists when the nurse says it's time to have her bath. She fights them, tries to rip off their glasses, pulls their hair. When the nurse lifts her into a wheelchair, my mother's feet start going a mile a minute as she mutters, "Gotta get going." She moves down the cement hallway. One day she went so fast that she careened into the wall the end of the hallway where a dozen ladies were sitting in their wheelchairs, like ducks on a pond, waiting for dinner. One of the white haired ladies extends her arm and her index finger, pointing at Mom saying, "She's… she's trouble." Apparently my mother took to calling the ladies in the dining room "bitches" and "whores". Her behavior got her barred from the dining room. I feel a strange sense of relief as I witness the whole scenario, like steam being released from a pressure valve. I realize that as a child there was no one I could tell that that my Mom was "trouble". Now a resident is proclaiming it publically. It's no longer a family secret. Crazy behavior is not just reserved for family members. Her polite social façade had cracked.

A string of visitors come to see my mother. One day Peggy, who becomes the self-appointed gatekeeper, announces their arrival, "Carol, dear, Emily is here to see you." Emily walks in wearing a proper suit of tweed, reeking of perfume.

"Uh-oh," I thought. She never liked Emily. "I wonder what will happen now?"

When Mom saw Emily, she rolls her eyes and makes a clicking noise with her tongue. Emily's oblivious. "Carol darling. It's so good to see you."

Mom rolls her eyes again and looks down with an "I wish you would leave" look on her face.

Emily's undaunted. She carries on relentlessly about her life, what their mutual friends are doing, the weather. After about ten minutes of no response from Mom, she politely says her goodbyes as though nothing unusual has happened between them. I guess by the way she hurriedly gathered up her purse and coat, that discomfort registered somewhere in her psyche.

Mother carried on about an old gentleman in the room next door saying he's her father. One afternoon I sit at my mother's bedside and she looks at me and says "Mother?"

"Oh no, not that again," I say to myself. My stomach turns. Flashbacks of being Mom's a helper, doctor, counselor, confidante run through my mind. No matter what I say or do to get her the help she needs, it's met with a string of "Yes, buts..." and a slew of excuses. When she asked me if the calcium lactate I had given her which cured her insomnia, had caused her cancer, that was the last straw. I'd had enough...Enough of role reversal, of trying to help, of being the good and dutiful daughter. I remember Eric Berne describing the game "Yes, but..." in *Games People Play*. I'm not willing to play that game anymore. Mom always insisted that she felt like I was her mother. I ask my good friend and wise counselor, Theresa, for support one afternoon, asking her to sit in on one of my phone conversations with Mom. I keep saying "No," over and over again to her requests to be her Doctor. I know it's not possible to be objective with a family member. She tells me to come visit her right away like other good daughters do, and ignores me when I tell her I can't because I have other plans. It doesn't sink in or make any difference.

Mom keeps telling me that she thinks I'm her mother and should help her right away. I protest, "Mom, I'm your daughter, not your mother. I can't help you. You need to go see another Doctor, counselor, etc."

"No, you are the only one who can help me," she pleaded.

"She's tough," Theresa said.

It took a long time to get my message across. I'm not sure I ever did. It just made Mom angry when I didn't slip into the compliant daughter role.

Back in her room, Mom looks past me into space and says, "Mother?"

"Do you see your Mother?" I ask.

She looks surprised, scared and becomes very restless. I put my hand on her chest. Her chest begins to heave. She lets out half chocked sobs. Suddenly, in sheer frustration, she flings her arms in the air like she wants to fight. As she struggles, I grab her hands and arms and follow her movement. She's strong and takes our arms went round and round in big circles. She fights furiously, making angry, frustrated grunts. Finally her head falls back on her pillow. Exhausted, she falls asleep.

This is the last time I see her.

About six months later, I get a call from Peggy saying. "Hospice says your mother is close to death. I ask my dear friend, Jerene, to go with me to the East Coast. She says "Yes," that she would like to get to know my family. She says she will fly from the Big Island. I leave from Maui, so we decide to meet in Chicago. I know my mother is living on borrowed time, so I call the Kirkland care unit from the Chicago airport. A nurse answers the phone, and then says she needs to go to find the woman in charge. After a long pause a voice says, "I'm so sorry. Didn't anyone tell you that your Mother passed away this afternoon?"

"No." I reply. I hang up the phone and search for Jerene. She embraces me. I weep.

If I could talk to my mother one more time,

I'd say to her, "I've longed for you to be real with me. It was hard to pretend everything was okay, when it wasn't. When I pretended, pushed away my feelings, I squashed my life force. I felt like screaming, wanted you to make some kind, any kind of real connection with me, wanted you to see me, hear me, connect with me."

When you said, "Put a smile on your face young lady." "What's the matter with you? " It must have been something you ate," I shut down, felt bad about myself.

The distance between us widened.

If I could talk to my mother one more time,

I'd tell her, "I wanted desperately to connect with something real in you. Anything. Not just, Did you brush your teeth? Comb your hair. It looks awful. How could someone who could look so attractive, make themselves look so ugly? Do your homework."

I wanted some crumb of love, longed to see acceptance in your eyes, hear it in your voice…not hatred and criticism.

If I could talk to my mother one more time

I would ask her, "Did we completely miss each other? Were there any moments of real connection between us?"

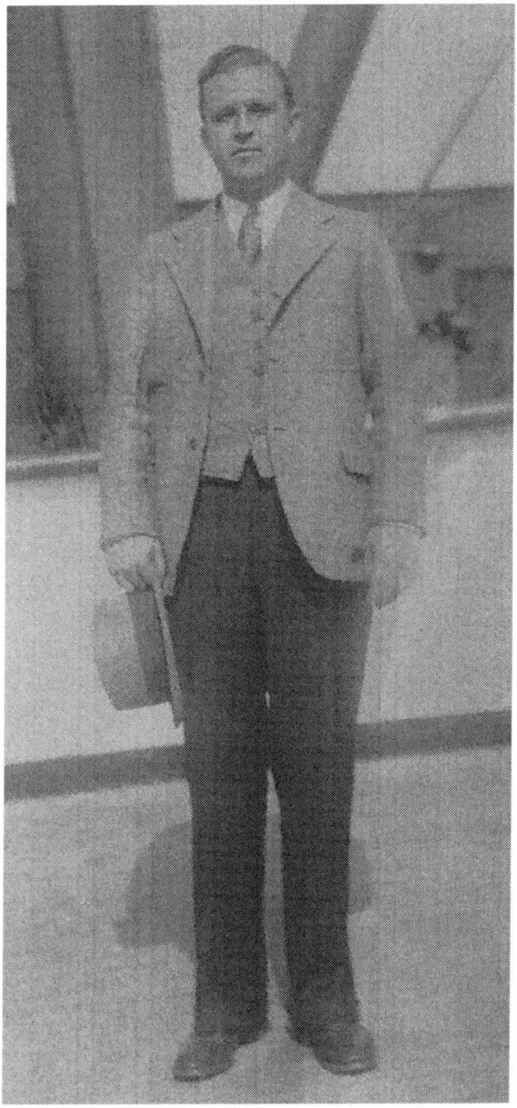

DADDY

When I was three or four
I idolized you Daddy,
told Mommy that
I wanted to marry a man like you.

When you didn't trust my words,
what I saw, what I heard
your pedestal slowly eroded,

I cringed at your castrating diatribes
and your drunken physical assaults.

I overlooked your meanness.

You traveled and left home a lot.
When you came home
you hid behind your newspaper,
spent endless hours at the office,
studied legal briefs in bed past midnight.

I wanted to believe that you cared.

Old Remnants – New Buds

When you came to LA on business,
didn't call,
my heart contracted again
my muscles armored
in anger.

I wanted you to love me.

Even when old age
bent your sturdy frame,
your eyesight failed,
you could barely move your neck,

I kept trying to connect with you.

The last time I saw you
and we said our goodbyes,
I moved next to your face, told you
"I've enjoyed being with you, Joe, even though you and Mom
fight and do the same old pattern."

You said, "Isn't that the truth!"
Your eyes became watery---
a lone crocodile tear
rolled down your left cheek.

MY FATHER AT 95

My father didn't say
        much of anything at all
        except
        this life is it.

My father
        was deeply depressed
        he thought he was his body
        and it was failing

He
        ate lunch and dinner in silence
        in the condo cafeteria
        slobbering on his bib

He said
        something terrible
        is going to happen in 2000

        that was the year he died

BRIGHT SUNNY DAY

My Dad used a boxing metaphor to describe his approach to life.

"You just got to get out there in the ring and fight."

And that's what he did until the day he died.

He fought and emerged victorious after a burst abdominal aorta and emergency surgery, survived an operation on his gall bladder and small intestines that were being strangled by scar tissue. When diagnosed with macular degeneration, he continued to read heady scientific articles with a large magnifier that had a bright light attached. When I was a kid he stayed up many nights past midnight reading legal briefs. He sued Minnesota Mining for patent infringement, and won.

In his late eighties and early nineties he fought against illness and death. I felt powerless as I watched his health decline but realized that there was nothing I could do to alleviate his suffering. First he broke his hip, then he tripped on his sneaker shoelace, fell and cracked his nose on the concrete pavement and injured his neck. He had to walk with a cane, then a walker. In the end he succumbed to a wheelchair.

The last time I saw him he sits in his wheelchair reading with a very bright light and magnifier. He's dressed in a tailored wool jacket, even though the heat in his apartment is set on high. He can barely turn his neck due to numerous neck injuries from playing football and soccer. When he sees me, he turns up his hearing aid. I move closer until I am right in front of his face. I have the feeling that I might not see him again.

"It's been good hanging out with you, Joe."

He nods, gives me a look of genuine delight as a lone tear makes its way down his flushed left cheek.

When I return home to Hawaii I call a friend who knows about Tibetan Buddhist practices for the dying.

"What does he believe in? Jesus? Buddha?"

"Nothing, he told me that he thinks this life is it."

"How do you think he would feel about a bright sunny day? Tell him that when he is ready to go, to gather all of his energy into his heart and then shoot it out of the top of his head into a bright sunny day."

"I don't think he'd buy that."

"He'll receive it anyway if you send it to him mentally or psychically. You'll know that it worked because his response to you will change."

The next time I phone him: a genuine, spontaneous, joyous quality to his voice, "How are you, darling?" Darling, wow, I like it. He even says he loves me just before we hung up.

I wake up at 3 A.M. on the day he died. I'm groggy, grumpy and irritated. I just want to go back to sleep. I finally decide to just relax into what I'm feeling: frustrated, lightheaded. As I settle down I feel a distinct presence in the room – a sense of my father. He appears to be delighted, and I hear his words exclaiming over and over again,

"I'm free! I'm free! I made it!"

Three hours later the phone rings. It's his secretary, "Your Dad passed away a few hours ago."

Rainbow photo by Katharine Stone Ayers

DAD'S FUNERAL

We step out of a black hearse into puddles of slush and ice…A cold wind blows through the Mausoleum. A hint of grey light comes through a jagged hole in a stained glass window.

I lean against the chest of my tall cousin Ted for support as I watch my dad's casket slide into a slot below his mother, who had a strange and toxic strangle hold on his mind.

Odd that he decided to be buried beneath her.

WE STAND

Katharine Stone Ayers

I LEARNED THAT

that you,
anything out there
will not bring me happiness

Now I see that I am the one
who allows happiness.

Alamanda photo by Katharine Stone Ayers

PINK ALAMANDA

You do not have to suffer in silence,
stay inside behind four dark walls.

You only have to step outside,
let the soft morning breeze caress your skin,
allow red leafed brush standing guard over the fishpond
warm your bones.

Look into the heart of the pink alamanda
be pulled into a center of chartreuse wonder.

Golden River watercolor by Katharine Stone Ayers

GRACE

Crusty old imprints from the past
collapse,
dissolve into a golden river

Old Remnants – New Buds

Joy bubbles through my heart

white clarity sparkles in my head

Rivers of effervescence

        move through my belly and pelvis.

Joy tempera watercolor by Katharine Stone Ayers

JOY

I want to write about Joy

Joy
kindled at five when Grandma invited me to pick yellow,
pink, orange, red roses in her backyard garden

Joy
burst forth when Uncle Pie taught me to ride the waves
at Wellfleet

Joy
of backrubs and jujube fights with teenage friends during
sleepovers

Joy
squashed by words
"Wipe that smile off your face."
"What are you so happy about?"

Joy
buried under a mound
of criticism, put downs, humiliation

Joy
frozen when I was raped violently at five
and again at sixteen

Old Remnants – New Buds

Joy
receded deep into my marrow when I was an object for
Mom's hatred
and Dad's lust

Joy
knowing that life has brought me angels and healers
who have helped me peel away layers of hurt and shame

Joy
returns like multicolored bubbles in my heart
and sparkles everywhere

Joy
that lay dormant, surfaces again

I am Joy.

Tree Fern photo by Katharine Stone Ayers

RAINBOW DROPS

Sunlight glitters on tree ferns.
Rainbow drops pour through my body
touching painful places.

I breathe
fresh warm rays that circulate,
flow
embrace my belly, muscles, thighs, heart, bones.
My brain is illuminated
with bright newness.

Old habits,
remnants of the past
slip away.

WHOSE LIFE AM I LIVING ANYWAY?

Should I keep putting everyone else first
and my needs last?

That's like Mom.

Should I be ashamed to tell
my women's group
that I can't keep my commitment
to give a presentation this Friday
because I feel like crap?

That's like Dad.

Shall I keep showing up when it doesn't serve me,
push the river?

That's like Mom and Dad.

Or run the extra mile,
do just one more thing,
even though I'm exhausted and in pain?

Yup, just like Mom and Dad.

Should I refrain from telling
Holly that she's fired
because I don't want to be
the bad guy
or hurt her feelings?

Expert training by Mom and Dad.

Old Remnants – New Buds

And what about Donna
who doesn't inform me
when she spends a fortune on plumbing
and a new water heater
without contacting me?

I think it's time to support myself and be real.

I say emphatically, **"NO!"**
to putting others needs before my own,
not speaking my truth,
not saying that I'm angry,
not taking a stand when I need to,
pushing myself beyond my limits.

Loyalty to the old family pattern.

I say **"NO!"** to that!

I say, **"YES!"**
I can take care of my needs first.
I can take precious care of myself.

I CAN speak my truth!

I can know that it is okay, even appropriate, to be angry at times.
I can say, **"YES "**
know and respect my boundaries and limits.

I can even enjoy standing up for myself.

I can say **YES** to LIVING MY LIFE.

YES! YES! YES!

Katharine Stone Ayers

YESTERDAY, TODAY AND NOW

Yesterday I was
the dutiful daughter,
heroine, helper,
took care of others needs.

Today I embrace
my humanness, weaknesses,
tiredness, overwhelm.

I take care of myself.

I connect with the earth,
feel support, warmth
affection.

*What matters to me
is surrendering,*

feeling the earth
beneath my belly

knowing I am separate from your pain,
your isolation,
your addictions,
your loneliness,
your living or dying,
your happiness or unhappiness,
your health or dis-ease.

*I'm relieved to know that I don't need to do anything
to make it different.*

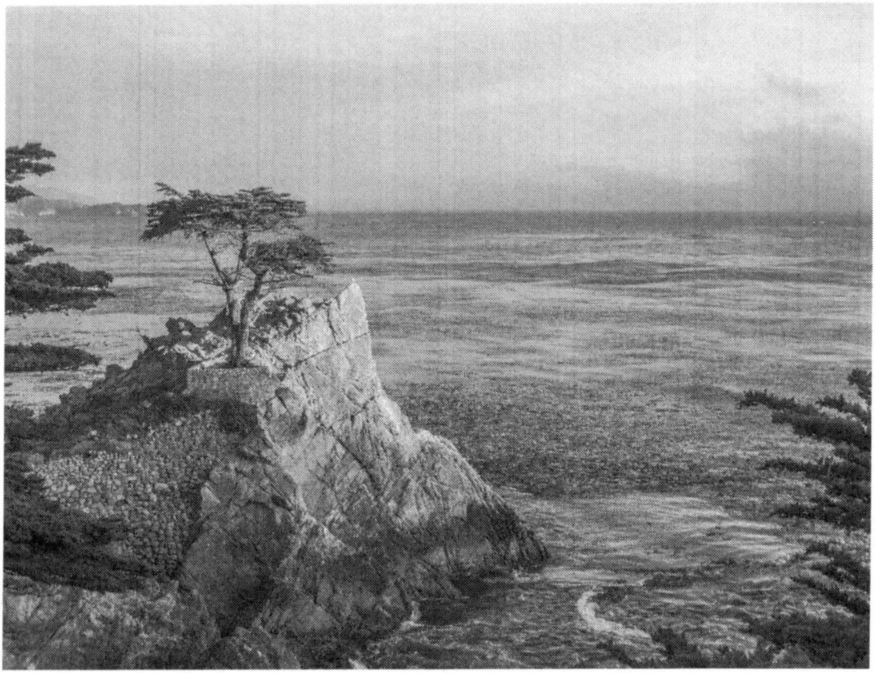

Katharine Stone Ayers

CYPRESS TREE

Small innocent babes.
You were not allowed to grow straight.

You were helpless then.

You became bent and crippled,
lived through
pain and deprivation.

Cypress tree,
so twisted, knarled,
you stand intrepidly
against barren rocky cliffs.

You are so beautiful!

Driving wind and rain,
relentless storms, sun beating against your branches,
have not destroyed you.

We stand
like a silent symphony
of elegance and grace.

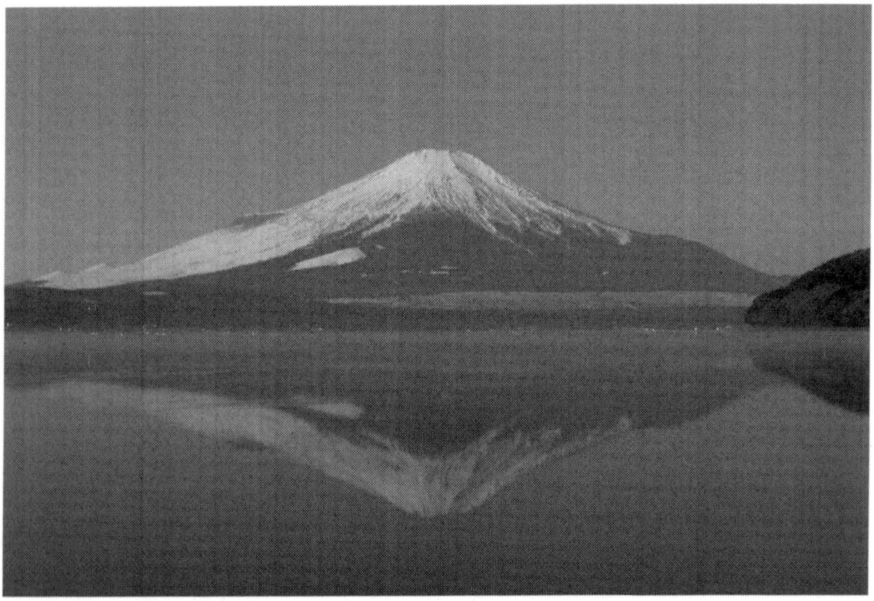

Katharine Stone Ayers

WAVES of CHANGE (From Hokusai's WAVE)

Waves of change
take me...
birth, death
marriage, divorce
radiant health, leukemia

Seeds, poppies, weeds
Giant red maple,
seed pods spiraling downward
like helicopters in the wind.

I stand resolute
like Mount Fuji.

Self Portrait oil painting by Katharine Stone Ayers

Katharine Stone Ayers

The sound of it makes me want to transform, allow an inner purity to emerge, become still, grounded, centered, go deep into the earth, fly away, dream, leave a legacy.

A name that wants to be said slowly, savored, rolled around on the tongue. Say it to connect to light, earth, wind. Dance it lightly, heavily, lyrically. Sing it in deep bass notes that resonate into your belly and toes, high notes that spiral lightly towards heaven. It tastes of water, earth, air, orange rinds. It smells earthy, ethereal, like rubies. Its colors are transparent like aquamarine. It whispers stories telling you to connect with yourself deeply, passionately.

Chant it from your heart.

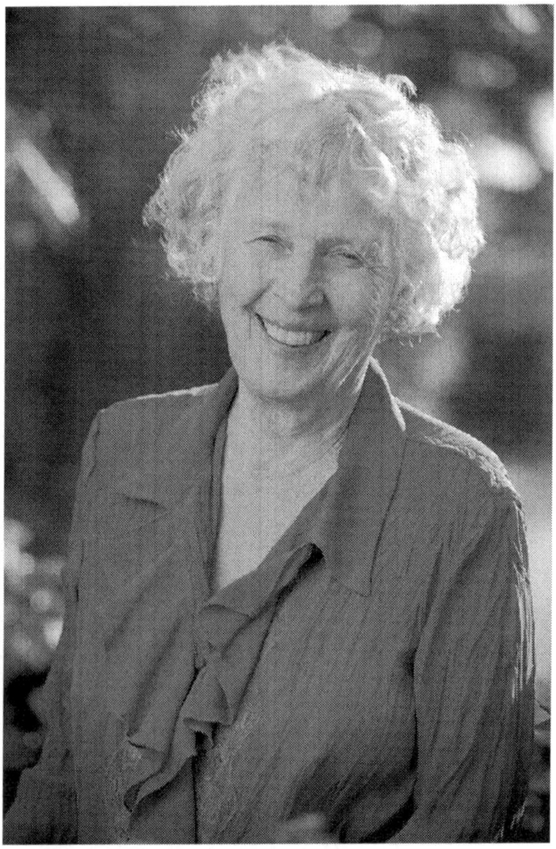

Katharine Stone Ayers

I WAS BORN TO

Open my ears to the sounds of the forest

Open my eyes to brilliant streaks of sunlight on the ocean horizon

Open my sensation to the magic of your touch

Open my nose to the scent of Uma's lamb curry

Open my taste to chocolate toffee sweetness

Open my life to each astonishing moment

Open my awareness to include everything

Katharine Stone Ayers

Golden dusk
embers fading
into purple stillness

Purple Stillness pastel painting by Katharine Stone Ayers

Katharine Stone Ayers

Silent reminiscing
setting sun
indigo and gold

Setting Sun photo by Katharine Stone Ayers

Made in the USA
Lexington, KY
10 December 2015